America: Heritage and Horizons

THE M. L. SEIDMAN MEMORIAL
TOWN HALL LECTURE SERIES

MEMPHIS STATE UNIVERSITY

The M. L. Seidman Memorial Town Hall Lecture Series was established by P . K . Seidman in memory of his late brother, M . L . Seidman, founder of the firm Seidman and Seidman, Certified Public Accountants.

Publication of this tenth Series of Seidman Lectures was made possible by a gift from Mr. P. K. Seidman to the Memphis State University Press.

The M. L. Seidman Memorial Town Hall Lecture Series

1966–67   *Financial Policies in Transition*
edited by Dr. Thomas O. Depperschmidt

1967–68   *The USSR in Today's World*
edited by Dr. Festus Justin Viser

1968–69   *The News Media—A Service and a Force*
edited by Dr. Festus Justin Viser

1969–70   *Taxation—Dollars and Sense*
edited by Dr. Festus Justin Viser

1970–71   *The University in Transition*
edited by Dr. Festus Justin Viser

1971–72   *China's Open Wall*
edited by Dr. Festus Justin Viser

1972–73   *Crime and Justice*
edited by Dr. Festus Justin Viser

1973–74   *The Social Conscience of Business*
edited by Dr. Phineas J. Sparer

1974–75   *The World Today*
edited by Dr. Phineas J. Sparer

America: Heritage and Horizons

edited by Phineas J. Sparer

MEMPHIS STATE UNIVERSITY PRESS　　　1976

Library of Congress Cataloging in Publication Data

Main entry under title:

America: heritage and horizons.

(The M. L. Seidman memorial town hall lecture
series; 1975–76)
    CONTENTS: Commager, H. S. First hundred years:
U. S. experience—Goldman, E. F. The U. S. experience:
the later years.—Montagu, A. America: present and future.
    1. United States—History—Addresses, essays,
lectures.   I. Sparer, Phineas J.   II. Commager,
Henry Steele, 1902–   First hundred years. 1976.
III. Goldman, Eric Frederick, 1915–   The U. S.
experience. 1976.   IV. Montagu, Ashley, 1905–
America. 1976.   V. Series.
E178.6.A39   973   76–30601
ISBN 0–87870–038–2

Contents

Preface and Acknowledgements   ix

Lecture One
"First Hundred Years – U.S. Experience"   1
by Henry Steele Commager

Lecture Two
"The U.S. Experience – The Later Years"   31
by Eric F. Goldman

Lecture Three
"America – Present and Future"   51
by Ashley Montagu

Coordinating Committee

FESTUS J. VISER, DIRECTOR
Professor of Economics
Memphis State University

ROBERT T. GARNETT, Assistant Director
Program Coordinator for
Public Service and Continuing Education
Memphis State University

FRANK R. AHLGREN
Retired Editor
Memphis Commercial Appeal

JERRY N. BOONE
Vice President for Academic Affairs
Memphis State University

FRED P. COOK
Operations Manager
WWEE Radio Station

MRS. CLARENCE H. FISHER
Member, Tennessee
Higher Education Commission

KURT F. FLEXNER
Chairman, Department of Economics
Memphis State University

ABE PLOUGH
Chairman of the Board
Plough, Inc.
Chairman of the Board
Schering-Plough Corporation

P. K. SEIDMAN
Partner
Seidman and Seidman CPA

BRUCE A. SPACEK
Partner
Seidman and Seidman CPA

PHINEAS J. SPARER
Emeritus Professor
College of Medicine
University of Tennessee Center for the
Health Sciences

America: Heritage and Horizons

Preface

The M. L. Seidman Memorial Town Hall Lecture Series in this Bicentennial year honors the United States' 200th birthday. For this historic occasion, the Coordinating Committee is proud to offer the theme: "America: Heritage and Horizons."

It is also with pride that mention is made that the current year is the decennium of the Lecture Series created as a living memorial to the late M. L. Seidman, oldest brother and founder of the firm Seidman and Seidman, Certified Public Accountants. Some special comments are apropos. The firm continues in M. L.'s tradition, an enviable reputation of both professional and community service.

Coming to the United States in his youth, and inspired by the venture, he at once started to learn the language and the ways of the new country. He obviously did not take "America, the Land of Opportunity" for granted. Being a pragmatist, although a youngster, he plunged avidly into nightschool study and daytime work. He was determined to uplift himself; to be a somebody; to do something important; to bring honor to his family, which he loved. He thus studied, worked, struggled and hoped for a future. This ambitious plan was first realized when he earned his Bachelor of Commercial Science degree from New York University School of Commerce; and he felt that the opportunity for an education had materialized into something excellent. Now he had to face the bigger challenge of applying his hard-won education to the rough and tough business world. He founded the firm of Seidman and Seidman.

Over the years, he revealed his great competence in difficult tasks and obtained distinguished positions and accolades in the field of his professional choice as accountant and in the related area of tax consultant, with special interest in taxation as a public issue. On several occasions, he served as consultant to congressional committees on taxation. Three New York governors, Smith, Roosevelt and Lehman, appointed him as delegate to conventions of the National Tax Association. He had important roles in both the American Institute of Certified Public Accountants and the New York State Society of Public Accountants. He served as Director and Executive Committee member of the New York Board of Trade, and was a member of the Taxation Committee of New York. He was a syndicated columnist for over 100 newspapers. He became noted as educator, consultant and author in his areas of special competence. Among his publications are professional and popular articles and the four volumes of Seidman's Legislative History of Federal Income Tax Laws that he coauthored.

The annual Memorial Town Hall Lecture Series in perpetuity is the benefaction of his youngest brother, P. K. Seidman, with the sponsorship of Memphis State University. The lectures attract a large general audience as well as students from the local colleges and universities. The students also benefit by additional classroom sessions with the lecturer as his schedule allows. The Lecture Series provides the Mid-South excellent non-partisan programs meriting public interest. It has been quite gratifying to the administrators and sponsor of the Lecture Series that the Memphis community has benefitted from them and has accordingly responded with increasing enthusiasm year after year.

For this year's Bicentennial Symposium of three lectures on the United States' history, the Coordinating

Committee was able to select incomparable speakers to discuss three integral parts of such a broad theme. Two of the selectees are professional historians, Dr. Henry Steele Commager, to review the United States' experience in the first 100 years, and Dr. Eric F. Goldman, the second 100 years; and a professional anthropologist, Dr. Ashley Montagu, to enquire into the enigmatic third century already at the threshold. He has also established himself as a venerable commentator on historical, biological, medical, social, psychological and humanitarian enquiries.

Except for Dr. Montagu, who read from typescript that required minimal editing, both Drs. Commager and Goldman spoke from brief notes that were modified and expanded during delivery at the time of the lecture, recorded on tape for subsequent transcription and reviewed by the editor for final publication.

Dr. Henry Steele Commager, one of the foremost historians of America and staunch champion of democracy, is a native of Pittsburgh, received his Ph.D. degree from the University of Chicago and did postgraduate study at the University of Copenhagen. He is now Simpson Lecturer at Amherst College, where he was also Simpson Professor of History and American Studies. Previously he was Professor of American History at Columbia, Oxford and Uppsala (Sweden), as well as professor or lecturer at other universities in the United States, Europe and Mexico. For the United States State Department, he served in many universities as special lecturer. He is a member of the United States Army War History Commission and a consultant to the United States Army. He has received several honorary doctor degrees, other honors, and membership in state and national historical associations.

He has authored and coauthored more than forty books, edited several others and has had scores of historical articles published. Among his books: Many people will recall "The Growth of the American Republic," coauthored with Samuel Eliot Morison, as one of the best short histories of our nation; "The Second World War"; with Allan Nevins "The Heritage of America"; Editor, "Documents of American History"; with Richard B. Morris as Editor in Chief "The New American Nation Series"; "The Rise of the American Nation"; "The Blue and the Gray"; and with Richard B. Morris, "The Spirit of Seventy-Six." In the field of historic interpretation and commentary, Commager's books include, among others: "Majority Rule and Minority Rights"; "The Commonwealth of Learning"; "The American Mind"; and "Freedom and Order."

Commager's lecture is a magnificent overview of the distinctive contributions in the first hundred years of our nation's Bicentennial, an event currently celebrated and vastly significant to our country and the world. For the most part, his talk deals with the founding of our democratic government, the newly established institutions, and the superb leadership at the country's helm. His breadth of view and depth of understanding survey and illuminate our nation's innovative and inventive contributions throughout that early period. He empathizes with the young country's leaders, at that time, with their particular problem-oriented approach to special questions, and with their daring spirit to prevail against kingdoms and empires of the old world, which were embroiled in maneuvers and intrigues to dominate and exploit the new world.

However, in the ever vital struggles for personal and ultimately national freedom, youthful America was blessed with a dual heritage: a grand leadership and an enlightened ideology, both of which were once and for all directed toward the common goal of first gaining independence and then of maintaining a viable democratic nation. The leadership and ideology, according to Commager, were heavily influenced by 18th Century enlightenment, i.e. Western ideology about fundamental aspects of human life, with reverence for the individual and society. Those profound principles confronted with or, more correctly, interacting with, the potent force of adaptation forged a model of basic cultural universals, first encompassed in the Declaration of Independence, then essentially in the Constitution and the Bill of Rights—all in the glorious enhancement of our nation's unique early development. Commager abounds with ardent praise, proudly done, in commemoration of those three American documents which, in time, were graced with the popular term "The Great American Dream." Though it has different meaning to different people, the American dream encompasses some core values, such as: access to education, pursuit of happiness, the ideals of liberty, freedom of worship, democracy, equality, individual rights, unlimited opportunity for improvement, progress and regard for love. Commager rightfully regards the Declaration of Independence as the glorious document of the American Revolution, wherein for the first time any people in history "let facts be submitted to a candid world," new premises for personal rights and the liberation of both oppressed men and government; and "that whenever any form of government becomes disruptive of these ends, it is the right of the people to alter or abolish it, and to institute new government . . . as to them shall seem most likely to effect their safety and happiness." By way of that document, it is also the first time for any people in history to be "appealing to the Supreme Judge of the World for the rectitude of our intentions ... and by authority of the good people of these colonies, solemnly publish and declare that these United Colonies are, and of right ought to be, free and independent states. ... And for the support of this Declaration, with a firm reliance on the protection of divine providence, we mutually pledge to each other our lives, our fortunes, and our sacred honor."

Amid such venture and virtue, "Our Forefathers brought forth a new nation," Commager asserts this was fundamental. Heretofore, nations evolved very slowly. He continues: "Nowadays we create new nations almost overnight ... the United States set the pattern for nation making ... within a single generation, imagine that, Americans not only provided for themselves the constitutional foundations, the political and administrative institutions, but provided likewise almost all of those other ingredients which go into the making of successful nationalism." He laments, however, our present plight, blunders and lack of moral leadership. He maintains that Americans of the 20th Century need to revive the spirit of innovation and creativity and to recover our sense of mission.

To quote Commager directly: "To find over again the boldness and the vision and the magnanimity which characterized that earlier generation. ... It has eroded almost completely in our own time when we created an empire not of reason, but an empire of power, an empire of force ... the defender of the status quo, the opponent of revolution everywhere." In contrast, Commager hails and marvels at early American ingenuity that bestowed so many extraordinary historic firsts, which he recites, in new forms and techniques of government, developed as national exigencies necessitated. Essential to the stability of the United States as a nation was the creation of an institutionalized, federal union.

In this connection, John Adams said that the United States "realized the theories of the wisest writers," that is, practiced them. Along the same vein, Commager states "The Europeans invented the Enlightenment and the Americans realized it. The Europeans imagined these achievements, the Americans institutionalized them." A written Constitution was established, with limitations on government and Commager compares it with the English and he points out that Americans only in recent years have had governments that sought to subvert the fundamental limits on government. He also compares the American Bill of Rights to the British counterparts. Furthermore judicial review was instituted in the United States and is still a unique phenomenon, existing only in our country, to overcome the inevitable tyranny of the majority and to protect the rights of the minority. All this makes interesting reading as does the discontinuances of colonies in our nation, which was accomplished, as Commager points out, by creating in their place new states out of the vast land that stretched to the Pacific; and admitting those new states to the United States on the basis of equality with the original states, as provided in the Congress and Resolution of 1780 and subsequent ordinances.

Several other innovations in the first century of our nation's history are also interesting to view through Commager's insight: The invention of the modern political party, in place of the previous political cliques, factions and gangs; the separation of Church and state by enactment in

1786 of Jefferson's Statute of Religious Freedoms. Its preamble also expresses ardent love of freedom of the mind; the establishment of the principle of supremacy of civil over the military power, with the provision that the Commander-in-Chief of the Armed Forces shall always be a civilian, the President of the United States; and the sense of fiduciary obligation to posterity, a sense that animated early generations of Americans and of considerable concern to Commager, who recognizes the difficulty of recovering that sense of obligation and the promotion of loyalty to posterity.

These contributions molded by the biography of our Founding Fathers and our other patriarchs into our nation's biography contain the core values that are our heritage or gifts out of the nation's past. They are regarded as hagiography, that is, as sacred writings though they were not designed by the will of God or divine providence. In reality, they are social creations, initiated and promoted by people, the culmination of a long procession of historical changes, as Commager explains. Thus, particular historical occurrences affected the American colonies, their people and leadership that led to the American Revolution, one of the memorable triad of 18th Century revolutions—the English Revolution, started about 1760 and became known as the Industrial Revolution since it was characterized by improvements in machine technology; the 1789 French Revolution, which was a stormy unsuccessful social revolution; and, above all, the American Revolution that newly created the United States and epitomized a new age, "an Empire of Reason" according to Commager, with ingenious, timely contributions in the furtherance of our nation's early progress. But since then and especially in the 20th century, he thinks, the United

States has drifted away from its most creative era, which needs to be revived.

Commager also has some concise, clear and worthwhile comments on several problems that are still current, though they first troubled or agonized Early America: *Happiness and progress*, he states, were not for the common man until we "look across the ocean to America," where men took them both for granted; in *Education*, he agrees with Jefferson that it is necessary to good government and the happiness of mankind and should forever be encouraged. Public education became part of the American philosophy and the great leveler; *Equality*, Commager considers intricately involved with both happiness and progress, all three quite close to our way of life from our country's beginning. He observes that Jefferson's dictum "All men are created equal "was advanced by the Age of Enlightenment as a fundamental law in nature. Only man and society resort to artificial classification, upon which inequality is contingent. Furthermore, theologically all human beings have the same divine progenitor, so none can claim superiority on that basis. But in contemporary American society, the concept of Equality refers to Equality of opportunity to all citizens, regardless of disparities among them in income, material welfare, living standards and in dignity of person.

Equality of opportunity, like love, is perceived as always capable, somehow or other, to overcome all sorts of barriers, restraints and inequities; the greater emphasis on *international cooperation*, which seems incongruous with the spirit of independence. But Commager is aware that Americans are now confronted with problems more grave than those that confronted Washington's generation; and that they cannot be solved independently by any one nation but by international cooperation, mutual interdependence serving the well-being and welfare of all nations, such as the problems of population, food, natural resources, environmental pollution, nuclear warfare, and *the critical problems of extreme nationalism* press for solution in a new light—the creation of an international community.

Commager concludes not on a note of despair but "encouragement." For, we have the natural and human resources and sound institutions, "if we preserve them"; and "a great heritage and tradition we can return to" and "moral standards." But what we really lack to perpetuate our proud heritage, he asserts, are "understanding and a leadership that will give us understanding" so essential in our world of disenchantment, terror and hope; and we need a vision that can regenerate our nation for "without a vision the people perish."

Dr. Eric F. Goldman, a most versatile figure in American academic life, was born in Washington, D.C., received his Ph.D. degree from The Johns Hopkins University, where he became a history instructor. He now is the prestigious Rollins Professor of Modern American History at Princeton University, and has written prize-winning historical volumes that continue to be required reading in many colleges. He has been a writer for *Time* magazine, has hosted an award-winning TV program, *The Open Mind.* His constant flow of popular magazine articles ranged through *American Heritage* to *Harper's* and *Holiday.* He was a regular reviewer for the *New York Times* Sunday Book Section. He served as member of the White House Staff, Special Consultant to President Johnson. He is the author of best-selling *The Tragedy of Lyndon Johnson*, which was syndicated here and abroad; *Rendezvous with Destiny; A property*" into the new idea of "life, liberty and *the pursuit of happiness*" celebrated in the Declaration of Independence as "unalienable rights." And Dr. Goldman continues: "So here is the heart of 'The Idea' and what a shimmering, crimson-shot idea . . . not merely an appeal for political democracy. It cut far, far deeper into the fundamentals of a man's whole conception of himself and of his relations with other human beings." As Dr. Goldman surveys his topic "The Idea" continues to be an intrinsic part of American history: in extension of voting without regard for having enough property, the wrong religion, or the wrong sex; the promotion of public education by a broad system of tax-support; increase of opportunities for the less advantaged citizens, especially status opportunities to the "blue-collar" citizens in contrast to the already favored "white-collar" line; provision of legislation for the "G.I. Bill of Rights," which created a boom in college students for the previously college-deprived by offering a war-veteran the right to financial support for further education or to a low cost loan to start a small business; and in the breakthrough known as the "Black-Revolution" and "Ethnic Revolution" that eliminated many discriminations against "minorities" and created, as Dr. Goldman states, "a revolution of expectations for ordinary Americans." "The Idea" behind the American Revolution seemed to be materializing to a wondrous degree." However, the early 1970s came, which Dr. Goldman characterizes as "a major watershed in the American experience," with three specifics shaking the new era—Vietnam, Watergate, and a unique recession. He mentions five basic American assumptions that were severely shaken in recent years: that the wonderful things accomplished by and believed in America are part of "an American Law of History"; our political

system is good, sound, practical; America is the land
of abundance; America does not discriminate against
"minorities"; and that America facilitates the upward mo-
bility of ethnics, having them participate in the main
stream of American life. Those assumptions, overcon-
sidered the essence of American democracy, were so
strained or shattered that they brought some tepid response and national malaise to the Bicentennial observance. Nevertheless, Dr. Goldman, like Dr. Commager,
remains hopeful and the reader of his lecture will be
pleased to learn the bases for it. His closing remark is truly
consoling: "It could represent not the decline of American
civilization but its maturing." Indeed, the maturing of
America as perceived by means of "The Idea"—"The
Idea" of America, perceived and idealized as America
really *ought* to be in the continuance course of its historic
mission.

Dr. Ashley Montagu, known to scholars and layfolk
alike, has a remarkable curriculum vitae suggestive of a
maturely civilized person. He came to the United States in
1927 from England, where he was born and received his
earlier education. In our country, he furthered his studies
and research in anthropology, first begun at the University
of London and continued at the British Museum of Natural History and the University of Florence. He served as
curator in physical anthropology at the Wellcome Historical Medical Museum and as assistant professor of
Anatomy at New York University. After earning his Ph.D.
degree at Columbia University, he became Associate Professor of Anatomy at Hahnenann Medical College and
Hospital, Philadelphia; then chairman of the Department
of Anthropology, Rutgers University. He also served as
visiting lecturer in the Social Science Department, Har-

vard; Senior Lecturer in the Veterans Administration
Post-graduate Training Program; Lecturer in the New
School of Social Research; Director of Research, New Jersey Commission of Physical Development and Health;
Visiting Professor, University of Delaware; and Regents
Professor, University of California at Santa Barbara. He
wrote, produced, financed, and directed the film *One
World or None.* He has been expert witness on legal and
scientific problems relating to human beings, consultant to
UNESCO and he has been responsible for drafting the
statement of race for that organization. He is a member of
several scientific and professional associations. The recipient of various awards, he is also known for his contributions to scientific and general publications, and for his
ability to popularize scientific and humanitarian inquiries.
He is the author of many books, among which are the
following: *On Being Human*; *Education and Human Relations*; *Man's Most Dangerous Myth*; *The Fallacy of Race*; *The
Cultured Man*; *The American Way of Life*; *The Humanization
of Man*; *Man in Process*; *The Biosocial Nature of Man*; *Touching, The Human Significance of the Skin*; and *The Natural Superiority of Women.*

Dr. Ashley Montagu completes this Bicentennial
symposium; and his topic is the United States Experience,
the Next 100 Years, which he chooses to name America:
Present and Future.

He begins his lecture by agreeing with Scott
Fitzgerald's depiction of America as a willingness of the
heart. But, Dr. Montagu adds: "And yet though the willingness of the heart is often there, we cannot help but
reflect that only too often there is a heartlessness behind
the show of heart." Then, the first part of the lecture
bristles to the brim with biting criticism of the United

what it ought to be." People, indeed make history but they do not make it de novo. They make it from what has been transmitted to them by the past, by what transpires in the present, and by what people project the future ought to be. Toward this goal, he commends "a revaluation of values concerning education." He quotes the noted British historian, H. G. Wells, that "Civilization is a race between education and disaster." And he quotes the Oxford English Dictionary, which defines education as "culture or development of powers, formation of character, as contrasted with the imparting of mere knowledge or skill." Montagu would, accordingly, "make the humanities the central core of every educational system, and all else devolve from that." Above all, the most important thing for a person to be is a humane being one having and showing love, kindness and tenderness. Accordingly, Montagu looks forward to America's history being uplifted by new generations truly educated, whose love and understanding will build an even better nation and a better humanity.

It should be noted that Dr. Montagu's views about education agree with many outstanding educators and educational philosophers as to the significance of education to the individual, society and to human progress; and in the best interests of those three considerations, education should aim to cultivate love, compassion and understanding of human beings, not merely to cultivate intelligence. When that kind of education or enculturation becomes universal, the cherished hope of Jefferson, it will elevate the well-being of the public in a democratically free country, and social progress could be expected to follow as a result. However, there are skeptics about this. Dr. Commager himself has written that "There is no assurance that education and freedom will in fact enable us to resolve those tremendous problems that loom upon us or assure a peaceful and prosperous future to mankind. But this is certain: that without education and freedom, it will be impossible to solve these or any problems."

In summarizing this impressive bicentenary symposium, some concluding comment is appropriate. The first thing to be noted is that each of the three parts of the symposium is not separate and independent but an intrinsic phase of a holistic, unified and ongoing historic experience encompassed by the revered name of the American Revolution. Truly a humane movement, from its very inception, it has been a harbinger of a new age in behalf of *the people*, "their safety and happiness," and "certain unalienable rights." That kind of American consciousness was soon reenforced and augumented principally by the Constitution and the Bill of Rights.

Our three guest lecturers are in agreement that those hallowed principles and aspirations have become national forces influencing the nation's politics, policies, and practices toward complete progress. In that regard, the civil rights revolution, among other social reforms, is far from being completed.

Distressed by our nation's paradoxical inhumane history, past and present, the lecturers articulate their convictions with rare candor and courage. They sense and verbalize an awareness that something is wrong in our country nowadays; a tense uneasiness, a moral "dis-ease" experienced by the people, who in their plight, are reaching for someone to make them hale and hearty.

In spite of misgivings, with America's *heritage* in eclipse and the *horizon* befogged, the lecturers have hope in the future for our democratic republic; hope that the third century will redeem America's pristine image and dream; and that the dynamic forces of history will be directed toward progress for all mankind. Such hope will be the fulfillment of new, genuinely educated and affectionate generations of Americans dedicated to humane living, and to the recognition of the role of *the people* in their government. Lincoln awesomely accentuated this role, in the Gettysburg address, when he said "that government of *the people*, by *the people*, for *the people* shall not perish from the earth."

As envisioned by the lecturers, the American people, through the government, has faced a critical problem in the new role of world leader since World War II ended. A nation's character is judged by the examples of its deeds rather than by what is professed in creeds. Example becomes crucial amid our contemporary agonized world, afflicted with frustrating dissent and cautious diplomacy, aggravated by the terrifying threat of nuclear warfare, making America's *horizon* ever precarious.

The guest speakers know they cannot expect Clio, the muse of history, to reveal to them the infallible course of action at any time. They do turn to us with hope to plead for an uplifting change in our core values: the qualities of love, compassion and education.

Acknowledgements

The Editor wishes to express sincere appreciation to all the people and institutions involved in the success of the current Lecture Series X. It is only possible to acknowledge a part of them by name. Without P. K. Seidman's kindness and financial role in the enterprise, there would be no such venture. As a participant of the Committee, besides, he has contributed much above and beyond the call of duty. Recognition is also due Memphis State University for sponsorship of the lecture series and to Dr. Billy M. Jones, President of Memphis State University, for his official and personal cooperation.

Thanks are due also to the guest speakers and to those who introduced them and presided at the lectures.

Special indebtedness and recognition are recorded here and go to Dr. Festus Viser, who as Director of the M. L. Seidman Memorial Town Hall Lectures, performs various strategic functions patiently as well as tactfully; and, likewise, also to the members of the Coordinating Committee, whose listing appears in the forepart of this book.

Special debts of gratitude for their contributions are also due the following people; Mrs. Reva Cook, who quite ably publicizes the lectures in the local news media, universities and in other suitable places; Mr. Robert Garnett, who is Dr. Viser's skilled assistant in charge of lecture hall arrangements; Dr. Robert S. Rutherford, who, as Director of Security at Memphis State University, safeguards the people attending the lectures as well as the premises; and Mrs. Barbara Lawhead, who efficiently transcribes the lecture tape material to typescript.

Lecture One

by Henry Steele Commager

When we think of the American Revolution, most of us think of it in terms of the Spirit of '76 and of that famous painting which celebrates the military. The Revolution meant the destruction of an empire; but far more important, it meant the creation of a new empire—a thought a generation of founding fathers like to call an Empire of Reason, an empire which was a product in many ways, not merely of British and American history, but of the whole Age of the Enlightenment, and which was to exemplify and to justify the Enlightenment.

It was incomparably the most creative era of our own history and politically the most creative era in the whole of history. And what needs to be revived above all is the creativity, the resourcefulness, the radicalism, the revolutionary sense of innovation, which we have so conspicuously lost in our own time. We can not but look back with astonishment on the fecundity of that generation, in the realm of politics, and constitutionalism and perhaps not less, of society as well. It is a sobering thought, I think, that every major political institution which we now have was invented before the year 1800, and that not one has been invented since the year 1800 and that the United States is still living on her political and constitutional capital, as she is indeed living to a very considerable certain extent, on her moral capital, inherited from that generation. It is high time I think that we added to these.

What is most astonishing I said was creativity. The first and most obvious thing that was created was the nation. Our fathers brought forth a new nation, and we take that for granted, but no other people had ever brought forth a new nation. Nations were not created; nations grew, century after century. Nowadays we create new nations almost overnight; that had not been true in the past, and the United States set the pattern for nation-making that was to attain development in the nineteenth century, though it differed very greatly from what which we have in the latter part of the twentieth century. Within a single generation, imagine that, Americans not only provided for themselves the constitutional foundations, the political and administrative institutions, but provided likewise all of those, or almost all of those other ingredients which go into the making of successful nationalism—the ingredients of common denominators: the common language, common school system, heroes and villians (alas, there were so few of those in that innocent day, we had to make do with George III and Benedict Arnold), with the symbols, with mottos, with the body of literature, now largely neglected but remarkable for a new people, with our own system of law, our own economy, with many other ingredients that go into nationalism, and with a common past which was created overnight. Indeed the past was a very special kind of past. We substituted to some extent the future for the past, that is the past that is yet to be.

The creation of the nation was fundamental. It needed fundamental institutions to provide for its character, its continuity, its effectiveness. How bring thirteen states, each believing it was sovereign, to work together for common purposes, to act as a nation? How deal with the vast territory to the west of the Allegheny? For the United States was born the last largest nation in the western world, and confronted at once with the problem that had confronted Euorpean nations for some centuries, with the problem of colonies.

The first of these problems was solved again, with extraordinary speed, by the creation of a federal union. We take all of these things for granted, but there had never before been a successful federal union. As late as 1862, the Regents Professor at Oxford, Edward Freeman, brought out a book called, *The History of Federalism from the Federations of Ancient Greece to the Destruction of the American Union*. A note on the title page reminded his readers that no federal system had ever survived—but the American did. There have been federacies like the Achaean league and a dozen others, the Lycean Federation in Asia Minor and so forth in ancient Greece, Federalisms in the Lombard League of Medieval Italy, or in Switzerland, the Helvetic Confederation, the Confederation of the Low Countries, the Hanseatic Confederation, even the British had had a stab at it, none of them worked. All federalisms were too strong at the center, or too strong in the parts. How were Americans to create a federal system? They did so with what seems, looking back upon it, consummate ease and remarkable speed. It was not all that easy, but it was done in a little over a decade. After all, we cannot create a world in anything like that today.

It was done by the solution of two problems. One which had historical roots. It was not so difficult. One which required an extraordinary degree of ingenuity. First, by the proper separation, of powers between the central and the local governments. That was arranged for in the Constitution, and arranged for so well that, with the exception of the great change made by the Civil War, it is fundamentally that distinction which we have to the present day, of the central or national and the local or state.

Far more difficult, was the problem of how to umpire the federal system, how to deal with the complex of issues that had destroyed all previous federal systems—discontent in the parts or tyranny at the center—and that problem was solved with great ingenuity by making the federal constitution the law of the land, and assigning to the judiciary the authority to umpire the federal system, a role which it still plays and plays well to this day; a role which it has consistently played only once has that failed at a time when everything failed, over the controversy about slavery in 1860 and '61.

Inextricably associated with the problem of federalism was that of colonialism: what to do with the vast territory to the west, territory which was doubled in 1803 and then, in the lifetime of those who fought in the Revolution or lived in it, was again increased westward to the Pacific. We do not realize that we were confronted at the very outset with the problem of colonialism. We do not realize the United States was the greatest colonizing power of the 19th Century because we have never called the territories from Ohio, Kentucky and Tennessee, westward

to the Pacific, colonies. We did not do so because we made
the right decisions. Other nations did not solve their colonial problems. In all other states, colonies existed for the
benefit of the Mother Country. That was taken for granted
almost everywhere. Even the most enlightened of empires,
that of the British, after all took that position. That was the
essence of mercantilism, and as late as 1766, you will recall,
Parliament passed the Declaratory Act stating that the
American colonies are, and of right ought to be, subordi-
nate unto the Crown and Parliament of Great Britain in all
cases whatsoever. No wonder Burke said, "No people is
going to be argued into slavery."

What to do with colonies? The Europeans did not
know and they have not known really till the 19th and 20th
Century. Just last year Portugal got rid of the last of her
colonies. The American Congress decided, wtihin four
years of the Declaration of Independence, that there
should be no colonies and Congress passed the famous
resolution providing that all territory given to the United
States should be formed into republican states and it did it
on terms of absolute equality with the original states, a
policy incorporated into the Northwest Ordinance and
followed without a break from that day to this; or at least
without a break, except for Texas which incorporated the
United States, rather than the other way round. Texas,
you know, came in on its own terms. But the result was we
had no colonial problem. We spread westward to the
Pacific with far less trouble than Britain has had with
Ireland alone, in the 19th and 20th century, or most other
powers have had with their colonies.

A fundamental problem that needed to be solved was
that of carrying out what the promise of the Declaration of
Independence proclaimed: governments *derive* their

power from the consent of the governed, the essence of democracy. Men make government and the men who make government can unmake government. Men have a right to alter or abolish government and to institute new government. *Derive, institute*—these terms are perhaps the most important in the Declaration except for the phrase about equality to which I want to return at a later time.

But how are men to make government? Nowhere in the western world did men make government. Nowhere had they made government. Though once again there should be a footnote for Iceland, which had a population of forty or fifty thousand that was self-governing. Aside from that, this theory which had bemused the minds of philosophers and dramatists from Ancient Greece on had not been carried into effect. The most remarkable thing about the United States of that generation is that Americans, in the words of John Adams, "Realized the theories of the wisest writers," and by "realized" it was meant, "put them into effect."

If we are to look at the whole of the western world, the whole of the era of the enlightenment, we can see the great significance was that Europeans invented the Enlightenment and the Americans realized it. Europeans imagined these achievements, Americans institutionalized them.

We perceive that, for the first time, we have institutionalized federalism, and institutionalized an accordant state, we proceeded to institutionalize democracy, which is the principle that government comes from below. There were antecedents here. The major antecedent was in religion and the first example of this in the New World was The Mayflower Compact where all the males on the Mayflower got together and drew up a compact of government that was drawn from the religious background of

Puritanism, Congregationalism, and of Separatism: that men can come together and make a church—they do not need the approval of a Bishop or a Pope, or a State. Where two or three are gathered in the name of the Lord, there they can set up a church. And Church and State were one, Church and Town were one. The notion that men could make government spread throughout the American Colonies: the Fundamental Articles of Connecticut Towns of 1639; the Compacts of Exeter; the Compacts in the Province Plantations; end in compacts along a series of frontiers—frontier after frontier, from those in early Kentucky in the 1740s to the Squatter Compacts in Iowa, to the Agreements signed by the settlers in Oregon along the banks of the Rolamit in the 1840s and the agreements of the Californians at the time of the Bear Flat Revolt—men and women taking into their own hands, primarily men, needless to say, authority to set up on their own, without waiting for permission from other countries. Archibald Henderson in 1774 led a number of North Carolinians westward across the mountains into Kentucky and Tennessee and he called them together from the little settlements of Boonesborough and Harrisburg and others and he addressed them: "If any doubt remained among you as to your right to write a constitution be pleased to remember the law of power is originally in the people and that you and you alone can exercise it." And this notion that power was in the people which is not a modern invention on the part of the young but deeply rooted in American political thought and above all in American political action was born of that era, it still remained to be institutionalized and it was institutionalized in a period of three or four years (you can almost say it was invented by John Adams himself who had a right to take out a patent on it if he wished to do so) with the invention of the Constitutional Convention, in some ways most remarkable institution to come out of the revolution; that Constitutional Convention which is so familiar to all of us. The Provincial Assembly of Massachusetts asked the people in their towns to gather together and decide whether they wanted a new constitution. All adult, white males, no qualifications of any other kind, were permitted to participate: the towns said they did, and sent delegates to Boston. The delegates, acting as agents of the sovereign people, drew up a constitution, indeed they drew up two, and both were rejected; they drew up a third, which was debated, word by word, clause by clause, article by article, in the towns of the state, and accepted. The first instance in all history of men creating their own governments with intelligence and acumen.

And the institution spread from state to state and is now a commonplace, as you all know, so common we are rather bored with the idea of a new Constitutional Convention, but it was a very great invention and it spread throughout the free and democratic part of the globe.

Government comes from below. All very well, but what of the government that comes from below? After all the war had been fought because Britain claimed to have all power over the colonies. How limit government? It's all very well to fall back on a phrase like that of Alexander Hamilton (surprising from Hamilton, who was not on the whole a romantic) that "We do not need to seek in the musty records of the past for the rights of man, they are written as by the Hand of God, with a sunbeam on the great face of nature." The sunbeam theory of constitution was not very easy for the British to understand, but it indicates something of the American notion that governments are bound by the laws of God. The notion that all government was bound is very old. Once again we go back to the philosophers of Athens, and perhaps of Judea as well, that after all God alone was the sovereign lawmaker. That what men did could never violate the will of the law of God and there were centuries therefore millenia of religious philosophy behind this notion that government is bound by the laws of God and it was to laws of Nature and of Nature's God that Jefferson referred.

In the Age of the Enlightenment something very remarkable happened. It was, it seems to me, the most exhilarating period in the history of Western Man and that was the Newtonian Revolution. The greatest intellectual revolution we know of in our own Western history. Men's minds were enraptured by a vision of a universe governed by law. The whole of the universe, of the Newtonian Universe, was governed by the same laws, the laws that controlled the movement of the stars and the heavens and the tides and the oceans, controlled the circulation of the blood in men. It controlled the rise and fall of empires. It controlled the economy, the law, society, art, letters, music. It controlled all of the activities of man. These were bound by the great laws of Nature and of Order.

What an exhilarating notion! But what it meant was that men could by the exercise of reason, apprehend the nature of cosmic laws and abide by them, and if we could persuade governments and persuade societies to conform to the laws of Nature and Nature's God they would progress, inevitably, toward perfection. This was the vision that excited the imaginations and inspired the ardent hopes of the Founding Fathers, that for the first time in history they would be able to achieve precisely this, and they were on the way, so they thought, to solve almost all the problems that had afflicted Mankind.

How limit government? Well, Americans were determined to do so and provided so many limits that we can only wonder the government could function at all in the early years of our history. There was a basic limit of the written Constitution which we take completely for granted, but no one else had written constitutions of governments except some of the American colonies who were not at all in the rest of the world. The written Constitution was itself a limitation, it set forth the terms of the contract. There was of course a federal system where the states limited the nation, and the nation limited the states. There was the separation of powers and even more important the equality of the three branches of the government. Once again something new in history. The British had developed the balance of powers, and Montesquieu thought that was a separation, but it was not, nor were the three branches of government, if there were indeed three, there were only two in English philosophy—the legislative power and the executive power, which embraced the judicial, of course, as everyone in Europe thought. These were not coordinate and equal. Americans were the first to create the system of separation of powers and the equality of powers, and with that elaborate checks and balances and short terms of office and added to the to the constitution's Bill of Rights, the first really effective Bill of Rights in all history. Once again antecedents, but antecedents contrasted with rather than compared with the American. The British had the Petition of Right of 1628 and the Bill of Rights of 1689, but the American Bill of Rights differed in two fundamental respects from these antecedents. First they were law; the British Bill of Rights were Parliamentary Acts. They could be overridden by any other Parliament, and you know what the Stuarts did to the provisions of the Petititon of Right and what happened to many of the guarantees of the Bill of Rights during the decade of the 1790s, in the period of British reaction. The American Bill of Rights were part of the Constitution, they were fundamental law. No Congress, no legislative body could override them. And second, they included for the first time not only procedural rights, guarantees of fair trial and so forth, but substantive rights. Freedom of religion, freedom of the press, freedom of speech, freedom of assembly, and in the states, many other practical substantive freedoms were guaranteed in the Bill of Rights of the Constitutions, including substantive grants of power (I shall touch later on the guarantee of the right to pursue and obtain happiness written into so many of the states' Bills of Rights).

Americans did succeed in placing limits on governments and those limits on the whole have held. Only once or twice in our history, most tragically, in recent years, have we had governments that sought to undermine and subvert those fundamental limits on government and to arrogate powers to government that were not to be found in the Constitution.

One phenomenon of limiting government, which is also a phenomenon in its own right, deserves special attention, that of judicial review, which was not so much invented as it developed. But it developed again, with extraordinary rapidity, from the 1780s on to 1803 when with "Marbury vs. Madison" it was integrated into the constitutional system. What an extraordinary phenomenon it is, this institution of judicial review, which exists nowhere else in the globe, in the way we now have it. What is most impressive about it, I think is, something not sufficiently appreciated. It was the first democratic self-governing people on the globe who imposed this limit upon themselves. The notion of the inevitable tyranny of the majority was a notion very widely entertained, even during the Revolutionary years. It reappeared again in Tocqueville's great book on democracy in America and it is a darling notion of reactionaries down to our own day. Here we have a phenomenon which flies almost in the face of logic that the first people to set up government on their own and to declare that the people have a right to have their will were also the first ones voluntarily to impose a limit on that will and to assign to the one non-elective branch of the government, the one branch of the government which had permanence of tenure, authority to limit what the other two democratic branches of the government did. That should always be kept in mind when we tend to think of democratic government as easy prey to mobocracy or to the tyranny of majority will.

One other major political institution emerged from this period, indeed, perhaps the major strictly political institution as distinct from constitutional, and that was needless to say the political party, so essential to the workings of the new government for the founding fathers, both state and federal, managed to set up admirable institutions of government and then went home. Somehow they had to be managed, they had to be worked, they had to be administered.

I say we invented the political party, we invented certainly the modern political party. There had been factions from the beginning of western history. It was factions that Washington warned against so solemnly in his farewell address; it was factions that the founding fathers feared above almost everything else, and well they might. They were deeply versed in history. They knew how factionalism destroyed Periclean Athens. They knew the history of factions in Republican Rome and in Imperial Rome; of the grave struggles of the Greens and the Blues in Byzantine Constantinople; of the Guelfs and the Ghibellines in the cities and states of Italy. The factions that tore France apart in the 16th and 17th centuries and the factions that were still so prominent in the governance and non-governance of Britain, even at that time.

Americans managed somehow to create parties which avoided most of the dangers of factionalism, and they created them pretty much in the model which they now have; the changes are quantitative perhaps rather than qualitative. First they created national parties, not local or sectional parties. How remarkable that was! To this day very few other countries have parties that are purely national; parties that are the common denominators of the whole people. Imagine if we had followed the road that other nations have followed even to this day. A Protestant Party, a Catholic Party, a Jewish Party, a Labor Party, an Agrarian Party, a Commercial Party, and a Banking Party, a Southern Party, a Mid-Western, a Western and a New England Party. Imagine if we had splintered our government as France, as Italy and so many European nations splintered their politics and their government. No, we created national parties and we created the two-party system not a multi-party system. We created non-ideological parties, parties that represented let us say the practical common sense of the American people, not theories. Again we take that for granted because that's what we're accustomed to though we like to use words like ideology and principle. Our presidential candidates today are always mouthing words like "ideologies" and "principles" though no one can tell what their principles are. Fundamentally, the function of parties is not to have ideological differences as we had once, 1860, and then look what happened to us. That was the one great division. Our parties address themselves to practical matters of policy, and of course, to such practical matters as particular kinds of leadership.

And the parties permitted dissent for the first time in history, not only permitted but legalized and dignified legitimate dissent; legitimate disloyalty if you will. They legitimized opposition. No other nation tolerated opposition. No communist or totalitarian nation today in the world tolerates opposition parties. It's inconceivable. No one did in 18th century Europe. The Americans from the beginning took for granted opposition parties, partly because they did not think the opposition would really be dangerous and destroy the Union.

These institutions, these creative acts in the realm of constitution and government did not exhaust the ingenuity or resourcefulness of that generation. In the eyes of the old world even more remarkable was the separation of Church and State. Once again look abroad. Nowhere in the old world was Church and State separated nor had they been. The Church and State were one. The monarch was the head of both. They were two sides of the same coin, the same shield. The Church supported the State; the State supported the Church; and both insisted on conformity, both routed out nonconformists and dissenters. Nowhere was there even the shadow of religious freedom, though Britain came closer to it than any nation except Holland. Even enlightened Holland which won the acclaim of contemporaries wasn't all that enlightened. The Dutch physician, Boerhaave and many of his disciples were the greatest teachers of medicine in 18th century Europe. Boerhaave was succeeded by a man acknowledged to be the greatest surgeon in Europe who was a Catholic. He wasn't allowed to take that post. He found a post in Vienna instead and Leyden University began a decline in medicine and surgery for some time as a result. The British thought of themselves as enlightened with respect to religion but they weren't enlightened toward the Irish. Nor were they enlightened for that matter toward most of the nonconformists. It's sobering to reflect that there were only two institutions of learning in England (there were four up in Scotland), Oxford and Cambridge, and that only an Anglican could attend and until 1871 only an Anglican could teach at Oxford and Cambridge. The others went without universities or went to the new growing municipal universities.

The Americans were the first free people to separate Church and State and to constitutionally establish religious freedom. That is one reason, there are other reasons as well, why we have never had religious wars in America; never had major religious persecutions. We are rightfully concerned when we have any form of religious persecution or intolerance—the intolerance towards the Catholics in the 1830s and 40s, the intolerance towards the Mormons in the 50s and 60s and 70s, the intolerance of anti-semitism in modern times, but compare this to what the Spaniards did to the Jews, Moors and others; what the French did to the Huguenots as they drove them out and destroyed them. Compare this to the religious wars which raged in central Europe for a hundred years, or the religious wars in Britain which raged again for a hundred years, or the pogroms in Poland or in Russia and other parts of the globe in modern times and the attitude of the Hitlerian regime towards Jews. We have miraculously avoided religious intolerance in large part because the Church was never involved with the State and our churches were voluntary.

The new nation of Americans established, too, the principle of supremacy of the civil over the military power, something very much at heart. Once again in the old world, military and civil were one. The monarch was head of the military as he was head of the civil. That same Frederick the Great who said, "My people and I have arrived at the amiable understanding. I allow them to say anything they want and they allow me to *do* anything that I want," didn't consult the people when he launched war after war throughout the whole of his regime: nor did George III think it was necessary to consult Parliament when he declared the American Colonies in a state of rebellion. Monarchs made war and monarchs made peace as best they could. Americans were determined to set up a nation, a series of states first and then a nation where the military could not usurp power and where the civilian authority would always be superior to the military. To this end, they wrote safeguards into the Constitution of the States and into the Constitution of the United States. That latter constitution ascribes to the Congress the power to declare war and to appropriate money for the conduct of war; and it provides that the Commander-in-Chief of the Armed Forces shall always be a civilian, the President of the United States, and it gives to the Senate, and indirectly to the Congress, a share in the conduct of foreign policy.

Something which even so astute a man as Mr. Kissinger either has forgotten or chooses to overlook.

Through good fortune the underprivileged came to the New World not the lords and ladies and dukes and princes. This created something like a classless society. A society more near socially democratic I suppose than any we have had in the 20th Century—far more so than any we have now. Always with the reminder that that was limited to the whites. Here was one conspicuous failure of that and of successive generations, the failure to deal with slavery. The shadow of slavery stretched across the whole of the land as it stretched across the whole of our history down to the present time. The one problem apparently insoluble. Many of the Founding Fathers, Jefferson, Rush, Rittenhaus, Jay and others, wore out their lives and their hearts trying to combat slavery, trying to eradicate slavery from America. They saw it was a cancer. As early as 1771 when he was still a very young man, Mr. Jefferson had pled in the courts of Virginia that slavery was illegal because it was contrary to the laws of nature and his plea was in effect thrown out of court. He returned to the attack again and again. He almost got rid of slavery in the whole of the West, but lost by one vote, and was able to get rid of slavery north of the Ohio River. At the very end of his life he could say, "I tremble for my country, when I remember that God is just and that his mercy cannot last forever and that when we come before the Judgment Seat we will have nothing to say for ourselves."

Jefferson's generation didn't solve the problem nor did later ones. It took the greatest war of the 19th century to end slavery and that war did not create equality. Not indeed for another hundred years was there political equality, not for a hundred and twenty-five years have we achieved economic and social equality. We cannot be too superior to the generation of the Founding Fathers in these matters.

Two other concepts rather than institutions command our attention. The concepts of happiness and the concepts of progress, closely allied. The 18th century was dazzled by the notion of progress and obsessed with the notion of happiness; the literature on these matters is overwhelming; progress was to be found always somewhere else. It couldn't be in Europe so it went into a thousand Utopian romances of one kind or another. Happiness might be found in any number of things. The happiness of your relationship with God and the Church, or the happiness of music and the arts and the great palaces and the gardens of literature and philosophy, the happiness of the disciples of Casanova in the amours so delicately portrayed in Boucher or Fragonard, or in the operas of Mozart which are also concerned very much with happiness. But happiness was not for everyone. It was for the upper classes, it was for the privileged groups. It didn't occur to anyone that the peasants had a right to happiness, or the children who worked in the fields, or who worked in the factories or elsewhere from the age of five up, or that they would understand happiness in any event.

And so too with the concept of progress. Progress was in the arts, philosophy, science, and in beauty; it was in almost anything but the welfare of the ordinary man. That was a wholly different affair. And even the Philosophes of the Old World—those deeply concerned with progress, those who again worked during the whole of their life on reform did not suppose that this had anything to do with the common man. The greatest philosopher of the 18th century, Immanual Kant, "Progress" he said, "if it is to ing Tennessee, provide in their constitution or the bill of rights that all men have the right to pursue and obtain happiness. If there are any young people here, members of the Memphis State University who find themselves unhappy, I remind them that they have a constitutional right, not only to pursue happiness but to obtain it and I suggest potentialities of a class action suit and I know who to sue if they are denied their fundamental constitutional right.

Happiness went along with progress and both of them involved equality and equality was something very close to the American philosophy and concept from our country's beginning. Equality, in Jefferson's meaning of the word and even for the Negro we do not fully take in the significance of this remarkable phrase: "all men are created equal." For we do not emphasize "created" sufficiently. This was not just an expression of hope or idealism; this was a statement of scientific fact! In the eyes of Nature and God all men are created equal, at the moment of birth they are equal. Nature does not distinguish between white and black and red and yellow. Nature does not distinguish, except for procreative purposes, between male and female, between rich and poor, between educated and illiterate. Society does. All inequalities flowed from society. So this was a very logical conclusion to come from the Age of the Enlightenment which held that men everywhere were the same and all differences were merely the accidents of history, the accidents of social or economic development. That, take off the clothing of society, quite literally, as well as figuratively, and you see how similar every human being is, that is the deeper significance of the wonderful observation of young Benjamin West of Pennsylvania who was sent over by his friends to learn painting in Rome (where else would one go in those days?)

and who was carried around by Cardinal Albani and the others to see the great sights and shown the Apollo Belvedere and burst out, "My God, how like a Mohawk Indian!" As indeed he was. That is why the Enlightenment adored the nude and why Romanticism which did not believe in equality, had adorned the nude. Take off the clothes and all men are the same. They are the same in mind and spirit as well as in body. And that generation firmly believed more than hoped, I think believed that it would be possible to achieve all of those ends—happiness, progress, equality, as well as the particular ends of the American Republic; and that generation had a right to thus believe. After all the auspices were favorable. Jefferson and his disciples, men like Rush, Rittenhaus, Tom Paine, Barlow, and others firmly believed for the first time in history men could prove what they were capable of. Man could be free from the tyranny of the State and the army, free from the Church and the ecclesiastic tyranny, free from the tyranny of war, of poverty, even of disease and ignorance for ours was the healthiest of societies where babies lived longer, men and women lived longer, suffered less than in the Old World. And education and the philosophy of education went along with all the rest of it. Jefferson was not only the greatest political philosopher but the greatest architect as well; and he had a number of other accomplishments that made him distinguished.

And all the auspices I said were, or seemed to be, hopeful. After all, here, as Jefferson said, "Was a country with land enough for our descendants to the thousandth and thousandth generation." What a remarkable phrase! And that when the Mississippi River was the western boundary! Here was land of such enormous abundance, as had never been known before; a guarantee that none the earlier generation. I suppose no word appears more often except the word "happiness" than the word "posterity." John Adams wrote to his wife, Abigail, the very day he signed the Declaration. "We may rue this day but posterity will rejoice in it." The sense of posterity that persuaded Jefferson to speak of the "thousandth and thousandth generation" is something that has gone wholly. It is tied up with the notion of land enough, of resources enough for future generations. No nation has used up its resources more rashly than we have; no people has exhausted its land and its forests and its soil and its fundamental resources more rapidly than we have and we've done so without concern for posterity. Can anyone imagine recent presidents speaking of posterity to the thousandth and thousandth generation while they urge the Congress to authorize twice as many nuclear bombs?

How we are to recover that sense is hard to say. Who is to recover, if we can, the habit of leadership, return to the realm of public enterprise what is now so largely confined to private enterprise. There's always the same talent in any hundred thousand or million people. Theoretically there are potentially so many jurists, so many musicians, so many inventors, so many men of letters, and so forth. It is society which pretty much determines what it wants to encourage. It was Salzburg society in the 18th century that encouraged music, it was the society of France in the 1870s, that encouraged painting. The specialty of the 18th century was political leadership. When you had a body politic of about 700,000, which was the adult male population of the United States in the 1770s and 80s, an adult male population that is not much larger than that of greater Memphis today and not nearly as large as that of Chicago, scattered widely throughout an enormous territory on a distant frontier without a single city over 35,000, with no great institutions, no great newspapers, no universities, no learned societies that amounted to much, none of the sophistication of Old World civilization the wonder is unfathomable: we produced Franklin and Washington, Jefferson ahd Hamilton, John Adams and Sam Adams, John Jay, James Wilson, John Marshall, Thomas Paine. We cannot produce any of those now in the realm of public affairs. The talent is here. It goes into science, it goes into jurisprudence perhaps, into scholarship, into the arts, and it goes into business and technology. It most conspicuously does not go into public affairs. And how we bring that talent back into the public arena, so that of 215 million people instead of 3 million, we can find the Washingtons and the Jeffersons and the Adamses, Madisons, and the John Marshalls—especially the John Marshalls. I am inclined to think, after the last decision of the Court, that is the problem to which we must address ourselves.

We are confronted now with problems more grave than those that confronted Washington's generation; perhaps more complicated. Certainly more grave and complicated in that we cannot solve them by ourselves. We are in the presence of another great watershed of history. A watershed which may indeed be the last watershed of our history. The distinguishing mark of it is elementary. It is that there are no longer any major problems that are national. All major problems are global. There are no longer any major problems that can be solved by one nation. All the great problems must be solved by international cooperation or not solved. This is true. You can make your own list. We all know the obvious ones: the problem of population which is expected to increase to over 7 billion by the year 2010; the problem of food, food enough to feed double the number of human beings on the earth; the problem of natural resources, resources of oil, resources of gas which may run out in forty or fifty years; the problem of preserving the resources of the oceans which will be the chief reliance for food and other things in the future and which are being destroyed by pollution of one kind or another; the problem of the pollution of the air, and the pollution of the streams and the lakes and the soil; and the problem above all of nuclear warfare with the prospect, almost unavoidable of the use of nuclear bombs in war. When the *Washington Post* on the first of January consulted the six leading atomic physicists in our country on their expectations of atomic war, all six agreed that there would be atomic war before the year 2000. The world was doing nothing to curb this and everything to move toward it; and the spread of atomic weapons into the hands of a dozen and soon a score of nations, the availability of the materials necessary to detonate atomic bombs in the hands of guerrillas like the Palestinians or any other, make it highly probable that a nuclear war would be under way within the next 25 years. Certainly the prospects are grim, and we are not moving toward a solution of that problem, rather the other way around.

How do we revive that earlier resourcefulness and ingenuity, that earlier sense of fiduciary obligation: that earlier sense of moral leadership which was ours? In the 18th and through a great deal of the 19th century in which we revealed again moral leadership as some of you are old enough to remember, in the Second World War, and in that most magnanimous of contributions, the Marshall Plan, which came to the rescue of the Old World and restored it.

If we are to achieve any of this there must be changes.

How they are to be brought about none of us know. There must be an abatement of traditional nationalism and of traditional concepts of sovereignty. Nationalism is today what States Rights was in 1778, 1787, or 1861. It is an anachronism, as States Rights then was an anachronism. National sovereignty, a fairly modern concept, is likewise an anachronism. If nations cannot solve these major problems by themselves and they cannot live, let us say, without the oil of other countries, what can they do with national control of these matters? There must, therefore, be construction and reconstruction of agencies of international cooperation, not from the top down I think but from the bottom up; a revival of the extraordinarily valuable special agencies of the United Nations which go on dealing with specific problems, not with the pride, vanity, ambition and aggression of nations but with questions of health, food, the sea, law, education and all the other practical things. In dealing with them across the boundary lines of nations as our scholars deal with national problems across the boundary lines of states, we must revive something of that notion of the great community of learning which animated the Age of the Enlightenment and which we are in danger of losing; that community of learning which realized that scientists, philosophers, scholars and artists have loyalty to their subject; loyalty to the search for truth and beauty; loyalty to posterity that takes precedence over any ordinary loyalties. That attitude which made it possible for the Royal Academy to give Benjamin Franklin its gold medal in 1778, made it possible for the Institut de France to give the English chemist, Sir Humphey Davy its gold medal in the year 1808 when France and England were locked in mortal combat and made it possible for Davy to cross the Channel and receive the gold medal from Napoleon.

That attitude which persuaded Thomas Jefferson to sit down in 1778—he was Governor of Virginia at the time and had given up his own beloved work in science, in literature and in the arts—and write to his friend in Philadelphia, David Rittenhouse, who was, after Franklin, the greatest American scientist serving Pennsylvania in time of war, to say he was fully aware of the honor it would do to our cause to know that Dr. Franklin and Dr. Rittenhouse were friends too, but he wished to remind them that there were higher obligations on men like Rittenhouse. "It is inconceivable," he said, "that nature would throw away a Newton up on the occupations of a crown. It would be a prodigality for which Nature, God himself, could not forgive, if he should be assigned to what was so far beneath him"; and he urged Rittenhouse to return to his scientific work. "Remember," he said, "the world has but one Rittenhouse and never had one before." Something of an exaggeration, but an exaggeration on the right side. We no longer think that scientists are exempt from the claims of nationalism. We have forgotten what the great smallpox doctor, Edward Jenner, said: "The sciences are never at war." He should have said the sciences *should* never be at war. In his day they were not. In our day, alas, they are.

We shall have to reconsider, I think, our own attitude toward science, our own attitude toward natural resources. We shall have to entertain the concept that neither our country nor the globe can permanently tolerate the control of natural resources of the earth by private persons or corporations. Nature, God if you will, did not necessarily give the oil to private corporations, nor the gas, nor any other thing beneath the soil. We sometimes forget that the notion of private ownership of these fundamental resources is a very modern notion. That up until the 17th century, indeed, until the 18th, it was taken for granted that the Crown or the State, the Sovereign, owned everything beneath the soil, not individuals. We should not bemuse ourselves with the notion that we can go on, that Western Europe and perhaps Russia, can go on indefinitely consuming three or four times our share of the wealth that is still here. We in America, with six percent of the world's population consume 40 percent of all the produce of the globe. And to suppose that fifty years from now starving hundreds of millions will sit amiably aside and watch a few nations like the United States, Japan, Britain or Germany live high on the hog while they starve is to imagine the inconceivable. To anyone who knows the power that will be in the hands of one who wishes to destroy the globe.

If we are to set any army on the road to the solution of any current problems then we must have a new international order comparable to the national order that we created—not comparable analogous I should say, to the national order we created in 1787. To do those things will require a revival of conservatism which has long languished or has been in disgrace in the United States; not the conservatism of the Old World; not the conservatism of Burke, which so bemuses the William Buckleys of this world; a conservatism which rested on the three foundations of the Church, the Monarchy and Antiquity. We do not have a church, a Monarchy, or Antiquity. We have old fashioned conservatism, and it is a great tradition. It is a conservatism of Thomas Jefferson, the greatest conservative in our history, who did more to conserve the soil and to conserve the dignity of men than anyone else, and it is the conservatism of Theodore Roosevelt and Franklin

Roosevelt, the greatest conservatives of modern American history.

For conservatism is not what those who mouth the word think it is. They do not know what conservatism is. The Goldwaters, the Reagans and the Fords have no notion of conservatism. They are describing "exploitative greed." Conservatism is fairly simple. It conserves three things. It conserves the soil and the natural resources for future generations. Even the soil on top of the mountains that strip-miners want to strip. It conserves the dignity of every human being and that is what is meant by Jefferson's "equality"; the dignity of good health, or access to it, of work, or availability of it; of justice which is the essential of every society; of education which the founding fathers thought was essential for the workings of democracy or indeed of any sound society. We have drifted very far from the recognition of the real meaning of conservatism. We no longer conserve our natural resources, we no longer conserve the dignity of every man, and woman and child in the country, of black as well as white, of poor as well as rich. We are in many respects an unequal society and an unjust society; unjust in the educational differences; unjust in the operation of the penal code; unjust in prison treatment; unjust in the health that is available to the rich and the poor; unjust in the housing; unjust in many other areas to which conservatism should address itself. It is a primary task of conservatism to restore nature and nature's bounty and to restore the dignity of man and to do this we must somehow, as I said earlier, revive leadership and how we go about reviving leadership is a very difficult task. We could perhaps make public enterprise as attractive as private enterprise. We could make public enterprise less unattractive and less costly if we meant to. But we do

not mean to. We spend just as much money now on elec-
tions as we did before. We do not think it is possible for
poor people to enter politics, only those who either have
money or who make commitments that will bind them
thereafter. When we do persuade people to enter politics,
we treat them pretty much as if they were criminals on trial
for misconduct all of their lives. It was Horace Greeley who
said he didn't know when he ran for the presidency in '72,
whether he was running for the presidency or the peniten-
tiary, and he thought the latter.

This is a large subject and I shall no longer enlarge
upon it. It is time for you to address yourself to me. I do
want to close however, not on a note of despair but on a
note of—I will not say "hope," that is too much—but
"encouragement." We do, after all, have great resources.
We have a population of 215 million, as well educated as
any other large population. We have sound institutions if
we preserve them. We have a great heritage and a great
tradition we can return to. We have moral standards. What
we lack is understanding; and a leadership that will give us
understanding. What we lack is a vision and without a
vision the people perish. Perhaps we should go to that
moving paragraph in Thomas Paine's last Crisis Paper. In
a recent address, Mr. Ford was quoting what he thought
was from *Common Sense* but it was the *Crisis*; but quoting it
on the side for further exploitation for everybody involved
and further armaments in which Mr. Tom Paine was not
interested. In the last of the Crisis Papers, he wrote:

"Never, I say, had a country so many openings to
happiness as this. Her setting out in life, like the rising of a
fair morning, was unclouded and promising. Her cause
was good. Her principles just and liberal. Her temper
serene and firm. Her conduct regulated by the nicest steps,

and everything about her wore the mark of honor. It is not every country (perhaps there is not another in the world) that can boast so fair an origin. Even the first settlement of America corresponds with the character of the Revolution. Rome, once the proud mistress of the universe, was originally a band of ruffians. Plunder and rapine made her rich, and her oppression of millions made her great. But America need never be ashamed to tell her birth, nor relate the stages by which she rose to empire. . . .

"It would be a circumstance ever to be lamented and never to be forgotten, were a single blot, from any cause whatever, suffered to fall on a revolution which to the end of time must be an honor to the age that accomplished it; and which has contributed more to enlighten the world, and diffuse a spirit of freedom and liberality among mankind, than any human event (if this may be called one) that ever preceded it. . . ."

Lecture Two

by Eric F. Goldman

I appreciate the compliment of appearing in the M. L. Seidman Memorial Lecture Series associated with Memphis State University. The series has established a reputation for being one of the nation's distinguished forums of free-wheeling and yet responsible thinking.

I'll try to repay the compliment of the invitation not by making a formal speech, full of pronunciamentoes and eternal wisdom, but rather by asking you to come with me, as it were, into the workshop of my own present thinking, some very tentative and troubled thinking indeed.

My focus, naturally, is the Bicentennial which, if it is to mean anything at all, calls for the long overview, the hour of inventory and stock-taking. In doing that, we must, I believe, start with a blunt statement. The Bicentennial is not a real success. It is closer to a disaster in the fundamental sense of the nature of the response it is provoking. There is even plenty of evidence that the Bicentennial observance is making many a thoughtful American feel downright uncomfortable.

Some of the reasons for this reaction are plain. Several months ago a former student of mine, knowing of my connection with the establishment of the national Bicentennial Commission, fixed an eye on me and said, "Sir, just what is there to celebrate?" It made me ponder. We are hardly in an exultant period of the Republic. Of just what shall we sing? Of Watergate and Vietnam? Of corruption in both political and corporate life making daily headlines? Of cities crumbling so fast that a recent mayor's conference warned of "oncoming disaster"? Of a public school system, for generations the life blood of this democracy, now descended to a level where a large proportion of high school graduates cannot read, cannot count, and cannot write a clear sentence? Of additional reports on the schools indicating that, to quote the *New York Times*, "crime and violence have become the norm throughout the nation"? Of a recession ending with a U. S. government prediction of at least 6% unemployment and 6% inflation extending into the late 1970's? Of an America the Beautiful from sewage-laden sea to shining oil slicks?

Then too, much of the Bicentennial celebration itself is enough to make wise men weep and so many of us, wise or not, wince. At times it is difficult to decide whether the worst is the rampant commercialization or the merely banal and ridiculous. Junk, junk, and more junk, James Michener sighs as he observes gaudy, shoddy "Minute Men" salt and pepper shakers. Up and down the country fife and drum corps, dressed in fake colonialism, fife and drum in celebration of events that were unimportant when they happened and have now reached a kind of higher meaninglessness. Books and pamphlets pour from the presses in unabashed vulgarity and silliness.

A President of the United States, later somewhat hectically retired to San Clemente, thought well of a plan for producing red, white and blue ice cream. We did produce red-white-and-blue toilet seats and "Bicentennial decked" coffins. A football league launched a $25,000 essay contest on the subject of the football league's relationship to the Bicentennial. Well, at least those essays ought to be short.

But all of this, dreary as it is, is not the basic explanation of the nation's reaction to the Bicentennial. Consider our first big birthday party, the Centennial of 1876. In that year the country was grinding through not merely a recession but a severe depression. In the White House sat the amiable, utterly ineffectual Ulysses S. Grant, long competing only with Warren Harding in historians' polls at the absolute bottom of American Presidents. Scandals in Grant's administration kept breaking month after month and in the fall of 1876 the United States had its one and only Presidential election which, beyond doubt, was literally bought. As for tacky commercialization, our genius for that was already in full flower. The James Micheners of 1876 had full reason to sigh as the 1876 tazzas and lambrequins burst across the country.

Yet this is the more important fact: The Centennial of 1876 was an unquestioned triumph. The public really responded. It was "the greatest, most enjoyable party the nation has ever given," one of its historians has written, "and one remembered long after many of the troubles of Grant's seedy years." The reason is simple: The center of the celebration was the Philadelphia Exposition and the actual official name of that was the "International Exhibi-

tion of Arts, Manufactures, and Products of the Soil an
Mine." In short, it was a spectacular array of the results o
technological genius in that period—primarily American—and it was an enormously impressive show, including everything from an elaborate assortment of nuts and
bolts of great ingenuity to the first patented systems for
dressmaking, on to the giant Corliss engine which was
revolutionizing industry at that time and of course to the
first public exhibition of the telephone. The observance
was complete down to its apocryphal story about the Emperor Dom Pedro of Brazil coming to the Centennial,
picking up Alexander Graham Bell's receiver, listening
and hearing words, and saying, "My God, it talks!" He
didn't say it, but it certainly was in the spirit of the
Centennial—that pride of Americans in technological
progress.

This, people were saying, is America's great achievement, invention, ingenuity, innovation that is going to
offer more and more economic and social opportunities to
more and more citizens. Americans have meant many
things by freedom but most especially they have meant the
freedom to get ahead in income and social status. Despite
the many unhappy circumstances of the 1870s, the public
could respond to the Centennial because the observance
was saluting one route for a national getting-ahead in a
way that seemed eminently realistic.

The Centennial, in its own way, was at the crux of the
meaning of the Declaration of Independence for 1876 or
1976. It was talking about and projecting what I am going
to call—to properly emphasize it—"The Idea" behind the
Declaration. Of course it is stated in the cathedral prose of
the Preamble itself. The trouble is we know that Preamble
so well we tend to glide over it, not realizing what we are

were to follow in the same or similar occupations and to live in much the same status. Upper-class families were expected to remain upper-class families. Now here is a document trumpeting: "*No.* Nothing has to be fixed about class lines. Everything is to be fluid; everything is to make plain"—in the words of an old American folk saying that came from the spirit of the Declaration—"There are no little people. They are as big as you are, whoever you are." The Declaration held up a vista of an unprecedented society, one in which ordinary men would walk in the tonic air of self-respect and could expect more and more income and status for themselves. More and more, and not only for themselves but especially for their children. No wonder the Declaration has proved a world force, exciting peoples on every continent, especially in the lands of Asia and Africa where society has been so frozen for so long.

In the United States The Idea was woven into American history and kept helping to bring about fundamental changes. To speak of the most basic fact, we started off a nation under the Constitution in which, as a result of state qualifications for voting, large numbers were disenfranchised because they did not have enough property or because they were of the wrong religion. It was The Idea of the Declaration, so powerful a catalytic, that did much to bring about in the early nineteenth century suffrage for all white males and then gradually extended it still further.

Or, in the early nineteenth century, the nation's few public schools gave few chances for an ordinary kid to get even an elementary education. The application of The Idea's central dynamic—opportunity to get ahead—was a principal factor in erecting the sweeping American system of tax-supported public education, first for elementary school, then high school, then college and graduate school.

Probably the most important influence of The Idea came when our nation after the Civil War entered rampant industrialization and urbanization. The whole "progressive," "liberal" reform movement that culminated in the New Deal amounted to an effort to use government on the federal, state and local levels to protect and extend opportunities for the less advantaged person. And it was Franklin Roosevelt, the climactic figure in it, who so appropriately said when asked to characterize his philosophy, "I'm a Democrat, an Episcopalian, and a follower of Thomas Jefferson."

The America of The Idea reached at least a temporary apogee in the years around 1960. We had a sheer economic boom such as no nation anytime, anywhere, had come anywhere near equaling. We had what might be called a prosperity psychosis in the United States—a whole generation, never having known depression, assuming that prosperity was the natural way of life. Something of the feeling of the Centennial of 1876 was being recreated by a new outburst of the brilliance of American technology. During World War II we invented what those of you in the business and engineering fields will recognize as "R & D"—"Research and Development," meaning that you take a hefty part of the profits of an industry and plow them back in order to mass produce new products. And we were getting conspicuous results from that, ones that conspicuously offered hope of constantly heightening standards of living.

Let me especially stress to you that around 1960 (I repeat "around," the specific date is just a convenient peg) we had a sense of an increase in status opportunities in this country again such as no people, anywhere, has ever known. It is necessary to distinguish between income and status. Sometimes in the United States they mean the same thing; having more money often gives you more status. Sometimes they're quite different. For example, in 1960 many American families preferred that their child become a supermarket assistant manager rather than a plumber, although the plumber might make considerably more money. The clue is in the status phrases "white collar" and "blue collar."

I discovered the other day in talking with a group of young people that the special meaning of the phrases seems somehow to be lost. Let me ask here of some of the younger members of the audience, Do "white collar" and "blue collar" have meaning for you? No? Yet for decades they have been a talisman of status—rising from the blue-collar group, where you work with your hands, to the white-collar group, where your hands remain clean and your tie stays on. Whatever the language may be today, the same status drive connoted by them has been and is a tremendous force in American life. To get across that white-collar line—ah, that was what millions sought—most particularly for their children. They worked for it, scrimped for it, spent a lifetime achieving it.

Some kinds of facts have a way of getting buried in history. One of them is a simple statistic of the year 1954. Then, the U. S. Government announced that for the first time in our history more Americans made their living from a "service job" rather than a "production job"—the white-collar job being that assistant manager of the supermarket or the person employed in teaching, the medical field, in sales, or the thousands of other non-manual tasks. With the general labor population of the United States shifting from production to service jobs, obviously many more felt the status satisfaction of being white-collar.

At the same time came the effects of a piece of legislation which, in its own way, has been the silent revolutionist of modern America. As World War II was being won, President Franklin Roosevelt faced the problem of the millions of veterans who would be returning to civilian life. After previous wars, the usual procedure had been to give veterans a money bonus. But that was not promising. Many veterans spent the money and wanted more; besides, there was the danger of mass unemployment. FDR's expert group worked out the basic concepts of legislation which came to be known as the "G.I. Bill of Rights." It has many provisions but the two most important gave a veteran the right to financial support for further education or to a low-cost loan to start a small business.

A number of experts believed most veterans would choose the low-cost loan; experts can be wrong. Overwhelmingly, veterans picked the further education. The Korean War came and Congress kept extending the G.I. Bill to more veterans. The legislation brought about what in many ways was the most important "status revolution" of modern American because if getting from blue-collar to white-collar was so important, the most generally assumed way to do it was to acquire a college education.

I know I speak to an audience of which, among the younger, there are many who do not think it remarkable that they are in a college though they may come from middle-class, lower middle-class, or ordinary worker backgrounds. Times have indeed changed. The simple fact of the matter is that until the G.I. Bill went into operation only a small percentage of families were able to send their children to college. College was a distinctly upper-class thing, and the nation was sharply divided between being the college and the non-college person. What the G.I. Bill did was to make a college degree possible for the masses; in case after case, the first person in long generations of an American family achieved an AB. Then he wanted to make sure that his children went to college. One of my more interesting experiences in Washington was to read some of the letters that had come in from G.I. AB's. Typically, they said, in effect, I'm the first one of my family who's a somebody and watch my children!

And then, in the years around 1960, there was the breakthrough of the minorities. When the word "minority" is used these days, it is often associated largely with blacks or Puerto Ricans. But percentage-wise, these groups were smaller "minorities" in the traditional American sense of the word. In longtime American usage, the majority, the so-called "typical American," has been a white, Protestant, Anglo-Saxon, "Anglo-Saxon" meaning generally a person of Western Europe origin. He was the WASP. And it was commonplace for discriminations to be made not only against people of color but against many millions of the other "minorities." One of the biggest of such "minorities" was created at the turn of the twentieth century by a huge flood of immigrants from southern and eastern Europe, most of whom were Catholics. The word "ethnic" may have its literal meaning but when it is used today, it usually refers to these Catholic migrants from southern and eastern Europe.

In a very real sense, American history has consisted of a broad canopy of economic and social opportunities into which new groups have been admitted or forced their way. At the beginnings, the canopy was occupied largely by

Englishmen and a few similar stocks. During the nineteenth and early twentieth centuries, the Irish and the Jews began claiming sizeable territory under the canopy for themselves. By the post-World War II period, the canopy was well occupied by all kinds of Americans but with two critically important groups still subjected to notable obstacles in their pursuit of income and status—the blacks and, to a much less but significant extent, the ethnics.

In the later post-World War II era, the years around 1960, came the breakthrough. Everyone talks of the "Black Revolution." There was also the "Ethnic Revolution." Typically, Vince Lombardi, an ethnic of Italian immigrant stock, had been a star, as you know, on the famous Fordham Rams, very football savvy, an extremely effective coach. But, as Lombardi would say, when it came time for the hiring of a bigtime coach, "they'd pick a WASP and Lombardi, because he was named L-O-M-B-A-R-D-I, would be the assistant coach." As the 1960s came in, Lombardi became the head coach of the Green Bay Packers and went on to his chosen glory. The exuberance of the ethnic breakthroughs was caught by another descendant of the turn-of-the-century migration, the ethnic bricklayer's son, Yogi Berra, who's a favorite of mine for many reasons. Berra was told that a Jew had been elected Mayor of Dublin, which was true, and he observed, "Only in America could such a thing happen." All over America, in occupations ranging from high executive posts in industry to the better secretarial jobs, ethnics enjoyed a new feeling of expanding acceptance and achievement.

Status breakthroughs, economic boom—the years around 1960 brought what must be called a revolution of expectations for ordinary Americans. The Idea behind the American Revolution seemed to be producing to a wondrous degree. Never, anywhere, had a nation expected so much of the present and future in terms of monetary real income, dignity and self-respect, and status.

Then, suddenly, it happened. I suspect that a hundred years from now, at the Tricentennial, historians will look back and declare the years of the early 1970s— more specifically, 1973–74—a major watershed in the American experience. Three specifics will be deemed the triggers of the new era—Vietnam, Watergate, and a special kind of recession. For what they did was to shake severely, if not to undermine, assumptions on which the revolution of expectations had rested.

I must be brief about these assumptions and omit entirely some of significance. One that cannot be omitted is this: The assumption that the world was going to let us alone while we did all these wonderful things for ourselves. We believed it so firmly that it was a kind of an American Law of History. Human beings everywhere and at all times want peace and democracy; they want to get ahead to middle-class living and by techniques that preserve the respectability of the middle-class way. Consequently the history of man is a long, slow swing to a world that consists entirely of middle-class democracies like ours. Once in a while trouble comes when an evil leader takes over a nation and forces it along a different path—the German Emperor of the World War I era or the fascists and Communists of more recent times. Then all we have to do is to slap such leaders down. With the imposters gone, the natural instincts of all people will take them along the way toward peace and middle-class democracy. Foreign policy itself is something we have, like measles, and get over with as quickly as possible. As I say, this was a very, very comforting Law of History. It meant that we were the future, we were on the right track, foreign peoples really weren't going to bother us for long. We could concentrate on the business of the revolution of expectations in America.

The headlines blared—the fall of Vietnam, in which we suffered a peculiarly humiliating and jolting defeat. It was only one, if the most serious, of a whole series of events in the early 1970s which shouted that much of the rest of the world was not interested in peace and middle-class democracy, even less in respectable ways of change, and still less in being an imitation of ourselves. In fact, some observers began to emphasize that this whole idea of a middle-class democracy is something quite new in the world, existing for only six or seven centuries in the 6,000 years of recorded history. Moreover, they were saying, "Today middle-class democracy is a little island in a vast sea of one kind or another of totalitarianism."

Assumption number two? We've assumed that our political system was a good, sound, workable one. Oh yes, there were always crooked politicians and stupid ones and ones who were woeful ciphers, but basically ours was a practical system. What we had not noted is that we'd been very lucky with respect to the part of the political system that mattered most, the Presidency. As some unheralded wag has said, "God takes care of fools, drunkards, and the United States." We have been extraordinarily lucky in the sense that out of the long line of Presidents—whom we persist in choosing in the most rococo of ways—we achieved ones who innocently presided over cesspools, like Warren Gamaliel Harding, the nothings such as Rutherford B. Hayes, the simply inadequate like a Zachary Taylor or a Calvin Coolidge. But the worst of them was tolerable. Then our luck ran out and we got Richard Nixon.

At first, still very sure of our political system, we told ourselves, Yes, we put the wrong man in, but look how effectively our system got rid of him. The House Judiciary Committee voted the impeachment counts, the Supreme Court ordered the White House tapes released, and Nixon had no choice but to be impeached or resign. But on second thought many an American was not so sure of our political system. What if Nixon had committed the same unlawful acts but not made tapes of his conversations? What if, when he first scented trouble, he had burned the tapes? How sound, really, was the American political system? The revelations of the dangerous activities of the FBI, the CIA, and other governmental agencies—all part of the general Watergate atmosphere—hardly tended to quiet the doubts and questionings. So again, another shaken assumption.

And what of the assumption that America was so much the land of abundance, so blessed with natural resources, that we could support an endlessly increasing standard of living? Of course you recall the sense of shock that went through the United States in 1973 when the Arabs clamped down their oil embargo. The effect of that too was permeative in American thinking and the worry was not diminished by the continuing evidence of other serious shortages or potential shortages.

Assumption number four—America and its "minorities." One group after another would be brought under the canopy of opportunity; gradually we would all be stirred in the Melting Pot and everybody would join in the Big Barbecue. No wonder we believed this so firmly; it had worked to a remarkable extent for almost two centuries. When the black revolution got under way, we assumed the process would continue for the blacks too. I remember laboring fervently in Washington on the civil rights legislation, the poverty program, and other governmental programs of the 1960s intended primarily to lift the black man. I was the typical American—I'm not attributing these assumptions only to other people, I'm attributing them in considerable measure to myself too. I assumed that if we gave the blacks adequate education, job training, a greater atmosphere of non-discrimination, it would be the same story. The black man would be like the Irishman, the Jew, and the ethnic and would move into the mainstream of American life with reasonable smoothness. Well, the jolt came in the late 1960s and early 1970s. Whether we weren't doing enough or whether the problem had different dimensions or both, the process was scarcely working well. It was, in fact, playing a considerable role in what everyone was calling the "urban crisis" and it gave a large section of the public the feeling that vital centers of the nation were disintegrating into shambles.

Finally, a fifth assumption, that there's endless room in America for an endless status striving. The millions go to college, the millions become white-collar. With the coming of the severe recession of 1973–75—and this is why I say it was a peculiar recession—we discovered that in a number of cities unemployment meant that some jobs were quite available but people did not want them; they wanted professional work. Yet in a number of fields we had too many professionals for the available openings. Take, for example, the law. This year we will graduate some 30,000 lawyers for some 15,000 openings. In general, as one scholar who has devoted his career to the ever more Americans; it said you should strive for it. Moreover, it never prescribed any particular level of expectations; it said you had a right to expectations, necessarily adjusted to the possibilities and problems of the era.

If you will think along these lines, you will note the extent to which today all kinds of new or at least different techniques are being discussed in all the troubled fields, whether education, foreign policy, or race relations. Many of the approaches are still in the thoroughly murky stage, but things are decidedly stirring. You will note too that, if these various discussions have any one common theme, certainly it is this: Let's cut down not on expectations but on the extent of the expectations which Americans had in the booming, soaring years around 1960.

No state was more a symbol of the-sky-is-the-limit than California. It is symbolic that California today has a governor, Edmund Brown, Jr.—I say this totally nonpolitically, he is not my candidate for President—whose chief theme is lowered expectations and who enjoys a whopping eighty-seven percent approval rating in his state. After all, you know, there was something a bit bombastic, frenetic, overly boomeroo and exuberant—like a very young man declaring that the world was his oyster—about the super expectations of 1960.

If in fact the present stirrings in America represent a search for changed techniques within the context of lowered expectations, we may simply be at another highly productive stage in the long and varied history of The Idea. Such a stage would hardly be inappropriate for the 200th anniversary. It could represent not the decline of American civilization but its maturing.

Lecture Three

by Ashley Montagu

It was Scott Fitzgerald who, with the simple sensibility of the innocent Adam, described America as a willingness of the heart. Without stopping to enquire whether it is possible to characterize a nation in so pristine a sentence, a good many of us, if not most of us, who know America fairly well would be inclined to agree with Fitzgerald. And yet, though the willingness of the heart is often there, we cannot help but reflect that only too often there is a heartlessness behind the show of heart, as when politicians kiss babies prior to election time and vote against free school lunches after they have been elected. Or when good patriotic Americans pledge allegiance to the flag "with liberty and justice for all," and deny those freedoms to Blacks.

Indeed there is so much wrong with America that many of its critics—and these are usually those who love America most—often forget to mention what is right with America. One of the principal reasons for this is that many critics feel a certain urgency, fearing that there is so much wrong with America that unless we do what is required quickly enough what is wrong will completely overwhelm what is right. We who have lived through the Age of the "Agenew and Nixtasy" as well as the post-Watergate period observe that practically nothing has been learned from those sorry proceedings.

Things, indeed, have come to such a pass in America that many people have given up reading the newspapers altogether, like the young man who said, "I've been reading so much about the evils of smoking that I've given up reading," because those who have given up reading find the daily reports of the moral breakdown of the country, the reports of crime, corruption, and injustice too depressing. America to them appears like a giant festering sore which infects and corrupts almost everything with which it comes in contact.

Corruption is, of course, nothing new in America. It is as old as the "discovery" of America by Columbus. The truth is that when Columbus started out on his voyage he did not know where he was going, when he got to what is now called America he did not know where he was, and when he returned to the point of his departure he did not know where he had been. It has been remarked that America has been in much the same state ever since. However that may be, the fact is that America's history has been corruptly written. For America was not discovered by Columbus. It was discovered and settled by the American Indians some 20,000 or more years before Columbus was born. More than three centuries of dishonor characterize our dealings with the American Indians whose societies and peoples we have for the most part destroyed and continue to these days in destroying. The corruption and

We have only recently concluded a ten-year iniquitous undeclared war, initiated by John Kennedy and greatly escalated on the basis of a deliberate lie created by Kennedy's successor in the Presidency, Lyndon Johnson, namely the "Tonkin Gulf incident," an incident which never occurred. This unimportant fact, however, did not prevent the whole of the United States Congress, with the exception of Senators Ernest Gruening and Wayne Morse, from voting in support of the Tonkin Gulf resolution. This vote committed the United States to a prolonged and utterly unjustified war which resulted in untold devastation and tragedy to millions of people, the loss of 50,000 young American men, and the scarring and wounding of scores of thousands of others. A war in which American soldiers engaged in atrocities on a huge scale, atrocities which were covered up by the higher command, which consistently lied to the public about body counts, alleged victories in the field, and on virtually every possible issue on which it was to their interest to do so. In which evidence of their malfeasance was deliberately destroyed, and to which every form of chicanery was resorted. Had it not been for a few independent journalists like Seymour Hirsch we would never have heard of My Lai, as we will probably never hear of the many other atrocities committed by American soldiers. The true extent of those atrocities will never be known to the public at large, even though most of them are known to many thousands of living Americans who participated in them, and have chosen to remain silent. These are the "heroes" of Messrs Agnew and Nixon and their kind, while those who conscientiously refused to be brainwashed into the atrocity that the Vietnam war was and declined to have anything to do with it, were penalized and to this day in the thousands

remember his previous political activities, especially as a
member of what will forever remain known as the "House
Un-American Committee," which spent most of its time
attempting to ruin the lives of persons whose politics it
found unacceptable. During the McCarthy period we
underwent the experience of seeing a junior senator from
Wisconsin making a career of lying, falsifying evidence,
and ruining the careers and lives of public servants whom
McCarthy labelled "communists or fellow travellers." We
observed the spectacle of innumerable politicians
applauding McCarthy and of President Eisenhower shaking his hand. Politicans like the late wizard of ooze, Everett
Dirksen, Senator Dirksen, Senator from the state of Il-
linois, a particularly egregious example of his kind, em-
bracing his friend Joe, as did, among many others, his
staunch defender and admirer, that other wizard of his
own special brand of ooze, William Buckley. Into this
atmosphere the Attorney-General Tom Clark had already
jumped during the Truman Administration with the publication of his list of possible communist front organizations. On this list was the Committee of the Arts, Sciences,
and Professions for the Re-Election of Roosevelt. This
committee was made up of many of the leading artists,
scientists, writers, and members of other professions. I
recall the names of subversive characters like Albert Ein-
stein, Harold Urey, I. I. Rabi, the celebrated Nobel prize
winner in Physics, Archibald MacLeish, Robert Sherwood,
John Steinbeck, Lillian Hellman, Katherine Hepburn,
Orson Welles, and innumerable others. The Attorney-
General's list was a thoroughly irresponsible and disgrace-
ful performance, which did not prevent it from serving
as an index for years for the excommunication and penali-
zation of almost everyone whose names were in any way as-

sociated with the listed organizations. Such persons were labeled either "disloyal" or "security risks" or both. In the name of "national security" good Americans have suffered from every kind of disability, vital information has been kept from the people, misdeeds concealed, and essential documents refused even to the Congress. In the name of "national security" giant corporations, especially oil companies have been granted national and international ripoff privileges. In this manner "national security" has become a euphemism for "national deception."

The language has become corrupted, as George Orwell predicted it would, by politicians and their minions. Words with formerly distinctive meanings have been rendered "inoperative." In Vietnam "Free Fire Zone" meant "shoot villagers and anything else that moves," "burn down everything—waste it." "Protective Reaction Strike" meant "drop large quantities of bombs on defenseless and other inhabited places." "Sanctuaries," meant "the invasion and destruction of Cambodia." In Washington "Executive Privilege" came to mean the above-the-law sanctity and Divine Right of Richard Nixon, President of the United States, the maintenance of Star Chamber proceedings and secrecy. "Law and Order" came to serve as a screen behind which every law and order was abrogated at the pleasure of those who conceived themselves to be not our elected representatives but our rulers. "Doublespeak" had, indeed, arrived not with a bang but a whimper—the whimper of the famous "Checkers" TV speech of Richard Milhous Nixon. As Orwell said, political speech and writings are largely the defense of the indefensible, and to quote him "politics itself is a mass of lies, folly, hatred and schizophrenia." Indeed, the corruption of politics has done more than anything else to debase the language to such an extent that its primary function of putting people in touch with one another threatens to be transformed into a means of alienation and deception.

The interference by the U. S. government in the internal affairs of other countries is now known to almost everyone all over the world. Let any group declare itself anti-communist and the U. S. will do everything in its power to support that group and encourage it to over-throw the legitimately elected government of the people. There are those among us who believe that is iniquitously wrong. Opposed as we are to every form of dictatorship we believe that no foreign government has the right to sub-vert the duly elected government the people have chosen for themselves. But this is exactly what our government attempted to do in Cuba. With our connivance the leader of the Chilean government, Dr. Allende, was murdered, and it developed in late 1975 Senate hearings that three unsuccessful schemes were launched by the CIA to mur-der Castro. In the name of intelligence gathering, the Central Intelligence Agency engages in the subversion of foreign governments and in the murder of leaders dis-pleasing to the government of the United States. That is, of course, a new definition of the criteria of intelligence gathering. It used to be said that if you look up any encyclopedia under "intelligence" you will find it defined in descending order of merit, as human intelligence, ani-mal intelligence, and military intelligence. We now have to add the even lower order of CIA intelligence. The CIA is not only sinister, it is incorrigibly stupid, for with all the largely wasted billions of dollars at its disposal it has man-aged to be both utterly misinformed as well as wholly unaware of impending events which anyone with a modi-cum of genuine intelligence and a reading acquaintance times written and discussed in the public media, but, again, no one does anything about these abuses. Companies like Lockheed ask for and are given subsidies of $250,000,000 of the taxpayers' money in order to carry on their business—a business they claim they could not carry on without such a subsidy, of millions of dollars which includes handing over large bribes to foreign intermediaries, and which are described as ordinary business expenses. Lockheed is only one of many American companies that have for years been involved in such corrupt practices. Some of us may call this corruption, but to the big corporations this is big business. And in one way or another corruption affects virtually every aspect of the business world, from the labor unions to the biggest corporations in the land.

The evidences of corruption are all about us. Hence, it is not surprising that almost every individual and institution in the land is to some extent affected by it. Our so-called educational system has become something of a shambles, as a consequence of the irreconcilability of what is taught in the classroom with what prevails in the world of reality. The young are especially severely affected by the hyprocrisy they see all about them, the pretension to creeds in ritually celebrated incantations, in which few really believe, the burning of incense before empty shrines. The young have lost respect for their elders, they reject their pretenses and their preachings, believing as they rightly do that the only measure of what anyone really believes is not what they say, but what they do. By that measure few individuals stack up well as adults, as parents, as a community. Young people have come to know their society as left without any moral compass by which to steer a course toward ends worth striving for. Lacking models whom they can respect other than those of their own age group, they desperately try whatever may hold out some promise as leading to a better life, today called a "lifestyle." Marijuana, drugs, sexual promiscuity, communes, clothes, language, music, and the rest represent a search to find some sort of meaning and humanity, of friendship and direction, in a world of conformity to the spacious, the immoral, and the establishmentarian. That the routes they have adventitiously taken to the New Dispensation are on the whole wrong, leading usually to the bleak windswept Isles of Illusion, only make the plight of the young even more poignant than it ever was. What they need is love, sympathy and understanding, not reproof or condemnation. They are right to object and protest against the values of their elders, those who in many cases have grown older without growing up, for these are the people who have in their eyes helped make the world the unhappy place it is. But they need guidance from those who can present them with designs for really creatively human lifestyles, and they are not finding such guides.

There is a massive failure of our society to do something about the problems that exist—not so much the problem of the compassless young as the problem of a society that so massively fails its young, and therefore itself and its future. Why, behind the show of concern is there so little actual involvement? Who should step into the breach if not the government, a government that is concerned about the welfare of the citizen—the need for the guidance of youth, the proper care of children, of parenting, yes, of being human. But, of course, the government will not do anything of the sort, and certainly with its present makeup and understanding of such matters, it would be most undesirable for it to intervene in these problems. The same could well be said of the community, but in that microcosm of the world it is conceivable, even possible, that a means may be found for the rescue not alone of the young, but through the informed endeavors of the community, the rescue of itself.

Many of us have become increasingly aware of the fact that we are not in full control of ourselves, that we seem to be driven by forces beyond our leashing. We have the feeling that we have lost all direction, in a world in which it is becoming daily more difficult to live. At the same time there has been a significant alteration in our reluctance to acknowledge the lowering of standards in virtually every aspect of our society, extending to both service and product, accompanied by the tendency to deny that anything has been lost with what has been gained. In this bicentennial year what we are in need of is not the empty ritual celebrations in which so many Americans will indulge nor yet ineffectual mourning for a promise that seems to have been lost. The best way in which we could render the American Revolution meaningful would be with the making of the only revolution that would be likely to save us and that is a revolution of values, of goals. If we are to have a revolution and revaluation of values and of goals then we ought to be quite clear what those values and goals should be. And we must know the reasons why. We must make quite certain that one folly is not replaced by another even worse. Toward that end it therefore becomes our obligation to acquaint ourselves with the best that has been thought, said, and done, and verified relating to the growth and development of the healthy human being in the healthy society. Surveying the history of humanity and the results of the last half century's relevant researches, I see the principle that emerges by which human beings better selves, and where we are now. Let us examine our strengths and our weaknesses, our successes and our failures, our real achievements and our shortcomings, with a view to holding on to what is sound, and righting what is wrong. I suggest that this become a national program, funded by the people through the funds they have already made available to government through taxation, more than eighty percent of which now goes down the drain called "Defense." The purpose of such a program would be to help each community throughout the land, with the assistance of experts, re-examine its values, and what requires to be done to change those values in order to transform the community into a healthy society. This would be a fascinating and a highly rewarding exercise involving every member of the community. I can think of no better constructive way in which to commemorate the bicentennial. There are enough women and men in our colleges and universities, as well as many other institutions, in addition to a good many outside them, who would be delighted to serve as advisors and moderators, not only as a service to their fellow-citizens, but in the hope that they could participate in producing significant social changes that could hardly be accomplished in any other way, and finally, because of the great and enlarging benefits they would themselves derive from such an experience.

People often ask "What is the future going to be like," as if the future were some arcane mystery, something that will autochthonously form itself out of some inchoate mass in some not too distant time. But that is mystification. The future is determined by one thing only, and that is, by what we do now—and there is nothing mysterious about that. If, then, we would like to see the future a different and a more decent one than our past has been, we have it in our power to make it so. Americans have made America what it is. Americans have the opportunity and the power to make it what it ought to be. "What is honored in a community," said Plato, "is likely to be cultivated there."

Hortatory appeals are all very well, but not of much help unless the words have practical meaning, unless the ideas are practically implemented, so let me spell out in plain English what I consider the necessary steps which must be taken if America is to become a land fit for human beings to live in. There should be a revaluation of values concerning education. Never were H. G. Wells' words more true than they are today: "Civilization is a race between education and disaster." It has more than once been said that education is the great American opportunity. But the question is, do we anywhere in America, or for that matter, anywhere else in the western world, have anything of that commodity, namely, education? With perhaps an occasional excentric exception, I think not. What passes for education is instruction—a training in the techniques and skills of the three "R's." When you get to college you learn the higher 3 R's, remedial reading, remedial writing, remedial arithmetic and then if you have the misfortune to be brought up in the land of perpetual pubescence, where they mistake cultural lag for renaissance: namely in California, you are exposed to a lower "3 R's": Reagen, Rafferty and the Regents' 27,500 students on each campus. And that is education. So there is no wonder that the first revolts on the part of the students started on the Berkeley campus, where a professor may speak to two thousand students who are not, of course, in the same room at the same time, because they have not a large enough auditorium, so he does not know their name and he does not recognize them and this is supposed to be the only in others, but also in the whole of nature—animate and inanimate, in all living creatures, and plants, and in the conservation and protection of the environment.

For the cultivation of mind and the formation of character teachers of cultivated mind and character are of the first order of importance. Recognizing this, those best endowed to become such teachers should receive the highest encouragements and the rewards commensurate with the value of the services they perform for the community. We in America do not believe in education. Because, if you want what people believe in, in spite of what they may say; it is what they do that they believe in, not what they say. What Americans do about education is to pay their educators about the lowest salaries that any profession receives in this country, much less of course, than the average truck driver but then truck drivers are far superior persons and in a democracy are considered at least as good as teachers. Put in more mundane terms, they should be the highest paid members of the community— beginning with kindergarten or nursery school teachers all the way through to university teachers. I would pay instructors in our colleges and universities more than full professors on the ground that the youngest teachers, those who are about to start their own families, are more in need of monetary rewards than professors who have completed those obligations.

I would make the humanities the central core of every educational system, and all else devolve from that. The humanities because the most important thing for a person to be in this life, beyond all other accomplishments, is a humane being. And as part of the humanities I would teach the art and science of being a warm, loving humane being. The ability to love must be the first requisite in a teacher, for the care of the student begins with caring for the student. The care of the patient begins with caring for the patient.

Had we not become so far removed from an understanding of what human beings are for we would surely never have made the mistake of identifying instruction with education. Instruction has a place, and an important one in the training in skills and techniques, but that place must always be secondary to education, the cultivation of the mental and moral capacities and character of the individual as a contributing member of society.

Will the future see a revaluation of education and its development along these lines or will such ideas simply remain an empty address to the supersonic layers of the atmosphere? The answers to those questions are that what will happen to such ideas will depend upon what we do about them now. If we go on as we have been doing in what is mis-called "education" and remain content with what we have rather than inspire new approaches, tested approaches, to the problem of education, it may be doubted whether there will be any future at all. For it is principally by raising up a new generation of human beings who sensitively understand what human beings are born as and what they are born for that we shall be able to establish a better society.

We fell into the slough of despond in which we find ourselves today in America largely because of our indifference to what it should be, and so we get what others choose to do with our abandonment. The enemies of humanity live on our weaknesses, not on our strengths. Human beings who are torn and distracted by internal insecurities and anxieties, who are conditioned to love their neighbors on Sundays and to compete with them on weekdays, cannot long survive. A nation of such individuals must eventually flounder on the submerged reefs of its own false values. External defenses can never make up for the lack of internal controls. Here, once more, the role of the teacher is paramount.

I am assuming here, of course, that what is required to make good human beings will not be accomplished in the home. The average American home is an institution for the production of mental illness in each of its members. Where the human beings of the future will be made is in the *schools*, and it is there where good parents will be made until such time at least when well made parents will be able to play the fundamental role.

Most people at the present time, in my view, are not qualified to be good parents. Parenthood is often confused with biological generation. That is another mistake. The parent of a child is the person who has parented it. The individuals who have generated the child are its genitors. Any Tom, Dick, or Mary can become a genitor—and, alas, most have—but to be a parent is quite another thing. It is only the most important role a human being can ever be called upon to undertake, the making of another human being. If that is so, then I suggest that it is time we consider the possibility that only those persons should be permitted to become parents who are qualified for the task. I would no longer issue marriage licenses, but at best only learner's permits. By this means we could achieve with a simple humanizing approach two things: first, the adequate preparation of society for the revised teaching in our schools of the new humanism (by keeping the population in the schools within reasonable bounds); and second, protecting children against the depredations of inadequate parents. A significant spinoff would be population control, parentage, and another would be the proper valuation of parentage, its obligations and responsibilities.

What are the principal requirements of the good parent? The answer is simple: fulfillment of the criteria of mental health, the ability to love, to work, to play, and to use one's mind critically—all of them qualities which the average individual is capable of developing. These are, of course, qualities which can be developed in the home, and our goal should be to help create homes where children learn to become mentally healthy human beings. Failing such homes, however, the school, the teacher in the classroom can to a very important extent serve to compensate for the deficiencies of the parents. How many human beings have been saved for humanity and notable achievement who would otherwise have been lost had it not been for a teacher who at the critical moment and for a durable period thereafter did the right thing which made in many cases the difference between life and death. There must be many such, for I know a goodly number within my own limited circle of friends. Good teachers can prepare children for good human relations, and what is parentage if not the practice of good human relations? Functioning in such roles, teachers will, indeed, stand *in loco parentis*, until we reach that stage in human development when parents can function as they ought.

Of course, we must endeavor to bring about the indicated changes in our society wherever and at whatever level we are able. Each of us cannot do everything, but we can do something, and what we can do is to help restore America to the splendid promise it once gave. Yes, America is promises and it is through making good on those promises through education, as the theory and prac-

tice of love—not the instruction which passes for education from which we suffer today—that I can see the only
hope for an American future, indeed, for the future of the
whole of humanity. It was John Adams who, in a letter to
his wife Abigail, wrote "Education has made a greater
difference between man and man than nature has between
man and brute." We would do well in commemorating the
revolution in which John Adams played so prominent and
significant a role, by pondering the meaning of his words
and deeds. Can we realize the promise of what John
Adams had in mind when he spoke of education? I think
that we can. Whether we will depends entirely upon what
each of us does about securing that great opportunity for
all Americans. And let us always remember there is no
promised land, only the promise we carry within ourselves.

1. James Michener, *Kent State*, New York, Random House, 1973.

2. See Ashley Montagu, *The Direction of Human Development*. Rev. ed.
New York, Hawthorn Books, 1970; also Ashley Montagu, *On Being
Human*. Rev. ed. New York, Hawthorn Books, 1970.